CLASSIC RUSSIAN IDYLLS

Frontispiece:

Ornamental Bridge at Tsarskoe Selo (now Pushkin)

CLASSIC RUSSIAN IDYLLS

Photographed and Edited by PROCTOR JONES

From Research and Translations of ANDREW WACHTEL

Introductions: ARMAND HAMMER

DONALD M. KENDALL

GERARD PIEL

Dedicated

to our grandchildren

and those of our friends

in the Soviet Union

Contents

Foreword

Rather than photograph people in the Soviet Union, I chose to reflect the atmosphere in which they live; atmosphere which inspired Russian writers, artists, and composers of other times. There is already a competent collection of Soviet social photography.

Among other writers in English, Suzanne and Robert Massie have framed Russian history for English-speaking people to understand. Mrs. Massie in her "Land of the Firebird" has told of art and artists, music and musicians, literature and writers. Mr. Massie's book on Peter the Great is classic. It is my hope that "Classic Russian Idylls" will visually complement such works.

The photographs record nature's excitement and reflect the language of great Russian writers. Research to accomplish this work has been carefully done by Andrew Wachtel, presently a Harvard Junior Fellow in Slavic languages and literature. Much of what we have printed here, based on his translations, is now seen for the first time in English.

It is our hope that "Classic Russian Idylls" will inspire appreciation of this area of the world and its people.

PROCTOR JONES

May 9, 1985, San Francisco

*In summer a bench in Moscow's
Filovsky Park is for lovers,
and with the snow and ice, a tree
is a perch for a winter bird.*

Introductions

DR. ARMAND HAMMER

Proctor Jones is the photographer we admire for being the sensitive poet we follow with delight along these Classic Russian Idylls.

As he did for "Idylls of France," the beautiful pictures offered to us are accompanied by texts chosen from works of great Russian writers and poets. Their reactions to the beauties of their land, their profound attachment to the natural environment in which they grew and their talent matured, make us better understand particularities of the Russian mind.

Because of the historical development of Russian culture and the structure of Russian society, writers and poets, artists and musicians remained much closer to their natural surroundings than in most other countries. The spell of vast untouched lands, the magic charm of changing seasons were always overwhelming inspirations, and the richness of Russian literature, music and art is a testimony to their vitality and strength.

For having discovered with his camera so many sources influencing Russian minds, Proctor Jones deserves our gratitude. Let us hope that a better mutual discernment of such sources of influence will bridge a better understanding between the minds of our two peoples.

Mountain Chapel in the Caucasus

DONALD M. KENDALL

Over the past twenty-five years, I have traveled extensively in the Soviet Union, even to far off corners that foreigners rarely have the opportunity to visit.

As a result, I have met many Russian people all over the Soviet Union and have developed some close and lasting friendships. The Russian people are great people. They are strong, courageous, competitive, and hospitable. Because of the political problems between the East and West, there is probably no group of people which is less known and less understood by us.

Mr. Jones is a photographer of breathtaking merit —with a multitude of stunning pictures ranging from an almost surrealistic misty snow scene to the colorful glory of a Crimean wheat field covered with poppies.

One of my favorites is an approaching summer storm that you can almost smell and feel.

But what makes this unique book even more so, is the coupling of this gift of pictorial painting with a wide range of Russian literary giants from Aksakov to Turgenev, authors and poets, whose words underscore the beauty of each picture, and open new avenues of interpretation.

Not only is this a beautiful book to be read and reread, but it is a book that I think will open our eyes and minds to a country that is so often seen in stereotype symbols.

Mr. Jones is to be congratulated, not only for a major photographic *tour de force*, but for a sensitivity that hopefully will bring people a little closer.

GERARD PIEL

There are photographs in this book that take us by surprise. In the far off land of Russia—farther off these days than the other side of the moon—we come upon a meadow, a turn in the stream, a path into the twilit forest where we have been before. The people who walk in these places must see what we see, hear the secret sound of the underbrush, feel the rush of recollection brought on by a scent from the humus. Since we know their land so well, why do we not know them?

Other photographs strike us with the strangeness and distance of Russia: the spindly birch and hemlock of the taiga, ancient pastures on a soaring mountain flank where we would find wilderness, a glint of sun on the gilded onion dome. These people have their own life and history to share with us, to recount and to explain.

A start on that sharing is given in this book. Passages from Russian writings appear on the pages facing the photographs. For us as for their countrymen, these poets, novelists, naturalists, revolutionaries, historians and scientists articulate in turn the wordless sentiment that stirs the heart and mind.

Sympathy proceeds to recognition. These people are as jealous as we of the singular individual existence given to each of us. They find fortitude in their inward vision of their country. They have our hope for the human species, and the inward vision gives substance to that.

If Russians have lived under tyrants, they have not been traduced or swindled by them. They survive to make the tyrants' monuments their own. Better than some people, Russians know that freedom can be killed only by its own hand.

By not knowing these fellow men, we place ourselves, as well as them, in jeopardy. With us they have the same stake in a world at peace. They are as beset as we by the prospectively irreversible consequences of stupidity and brutality empowered by national states with nuclear weapons in their arsenals. Our mutual security calls us to understand one another.

About the Authors

Russian writers have always celebrated the natural and man-made beauty of their homeland. In selecting texts to accompany photographs in this work, the attempt was to find quotations that would either evoke the same feelings as those suggested by the photograph or that would give the reader an informative description of an unfamiliar place. Some of this material is available in other English translations, much of it has never been translated before. Whenever possible quotations are chosen from works of literature because the photographs depict precisely those Russian scenes that inspired the greatest Russian writers, musicians and artists.

The passages range from the medieval legend of the city of Kitezh to the stories of Shukshin, Bitov and Soloukhin of the 1960s and 70s. The majority of the literature, however, was excerpted from the work of those 19th- and 20th-century writers whose work gave Russian literature a position of honor in world literature: Pushkin, Gogol', Lermontov, Turgenev, Tolstoy, Dostoevsky, Pasternak, Mandelshtam and Tsvetaeva. These writers were intimately familiar with the beauty of their surroundings and wrote about them with power and love.

Our route stretched almost 3,000 miles from north to south and 1,500 miles from east to west. So did the experience of Russian writers. Tolstoy and Turgenev grew up amidst the pastoral beauty of central Russia. Pushkin, Lermontov, Tolstoy, Pasternak and Mandelshtam traveled through the wild mountain landscapes of the Caucasus. All of them knew the country's major cities.

In addition to famous writers, many travelers, both Western European and Russian, journeyed through Russia and the Soviet Union. Their descriptions, while generally lacking the poetic qualities of the literary passages, are more precise and act as a counterbalance to the more evocative quotations. What is surprising to the modern traveler is that, despite the changes wrought by revolution, war and modernization, a great deal of what these observers saw is still visible today.

ANDREW WACHTEL

Farmhouse at Suzdal

A Word from the Photographer

A publication of this nature obviously involves many more persons than the operator of the camera. Without the very substantial assistance of Andrew Wachtel and my son Proctor,* this would have taken a much longer time to produce.

Alcxander Potemkin, of the Soviet Consulate General in San Francisco, was the first to suggest the project, seconded by Consul General Alexander D. Chikvaidze. Since that time, members of the Consulate have been most helpful in the planning. Consul General Anatoly G. Myshkov provided introductions which proved helpful. The Chief of the Novosti Press Section at the Soviet Embassy, Oleg P. Benyukh, made arrangements for full cooperation from that agency's headquarters through the offices of Oleg Shibko and Eugene A. Zykov.

Most of the time we traveled by ourselves but were aided, upon request, by Sergei S. Ivanko, Deputy Chairman of Novosti Press in Moscow, and his assistant, Sergei Nikitenko. We were helped in the field by Leonid Shiryaev, Sergei Kharchenko, Vladimir Kolinko, Igor Zaseda, Alla Belyakova, and David Imedashvili. These people shared their knowledge and experience with us, never once intruding on our creative efforts or denying our requests.

All seemed to appreciate that an American wanted to reflect for his countrymen the beauty of their native land.

The three distinguished gentlemen who honored this work with the writing of an introduction have long been interested in Soviet-American understanding. I am deeply grateful to Dr. Armand Hammer, Chairman of the Board and Chief Executive Officer of Occidental Petroleum Corporation, Mr. Donald M.

*I'm grateful for his photographs on pages 7, 57, 61, 63, 79, 90, 111.

Kendall, Chairman and Chief Executive Officer of PepsiCo, Inc., and Mr. Gerard Piel, Chairman of the Board of Scientific American.

Mars, Inc. of Hackettstown, N.J., through Forest Mars, a friend of former President Mikoyan, provided us with enough M&M's (peanut) to make a legion of Soviet children happy.

Diana Nichols, of my staff, patiently typed and proofed all of the material, a job made difficult by unfamiliar names and spellings. She was ably assisted by Victoria Carlyle.

To Adrian Wilson we are indebted for the classic design of the work, and we are also indebted to our friends, Frank Scott, Estelle Caen Barrett, Jean and Irving Stone for their continued encouragement of the project. Edmond Gross prepared and supervised the production with an efficiency that has made early publication possible.

Because of what I thought might be arduous travel, my wife Martha did not accompany us. For her patience during our absences, I am most grateful and just a little bit guilty, as I discovered the travel was not so arduous. I am even more grateful for her faith in the project which gave us strength in moments when encouragement was most needed.

The Dedication embraces our grandchildren and those of our Soviet friends. It came about during an interview accorded me in Moscow when the interviewer, Mrs. Marina Amarova, an attractive newswoman, told me that she had grandchildren too. She was deeply moved when I told her that this work would be dedicated to her grandchildren and ours.

The Moscow River and the Kremlin

Now, at leisure, won't you walk with me to the
Kremlin? At each step along the way I will exclaim
involuntarily: it is a mammoth city built by giants;
tower upon tower, wall upon wall, palace next to
palace! A strange mixture of ancient and modern
architecture, poverty and riches, European morals
and Eastern customs! A wonderful, incomprehensible
synthesis of conceit, vanity, and true glory and
magnificence, ignorance and enlightenment, civiliza-
tion and barbarism. Don't be amazed, my friend:
Moscow is a symbol or a living picture of our
fatherland. . . . We look again at the Kremlin whose
golden domes and belltower spires reflect the brightly
shining sunset. The city's hum dies down with
the dying day.

K. N. BATYUSHKOV, *A Walk Around Moscow*, 1812

*A thousand years of history
beside the ice-laden Moscow River.*

Entrance to Red Square

What can be compared to this Kremlin that stands on a high hill, like the sovereign crown on the brow of a stern ruler, surrounded by crenellated walls and ornamented with the golden towers of cathedrals?

It is Russia's altar and many sacrifices worthy of the fatherland must be, and have already been, carried out thereon.

What is more majestic than these gloomy temples, crowded together in a single pile, than this mysterious palace of Godunov, raised up like a sepulchral mausoleum amid a desert in memory of great tsars, whose cold columns and slabs have not heard the sounds of a human voice for so many years? . . .

No, it is not possible to describe the Kremlin, its crenellated walls, its dark passageways, its splendid palaces. . . . You must see, see . . . you must feel everything that it says to the heart and the imagination.

M. Yu. LERMONTOV, *A Panorama of Moscow*, 1834

It is an exciting experience to visit Red Square in the middle of the night, winter or summer. It is a private visit to centuries of history.

The Church of the Tikhvinsky Mother of God, Moscow

Once, on a day off, Stepka went to the church again.
He sat on a hillside and began to look at it carefully.
Peace and quiet all around. Quiet in the village.
And the white beauty stands there—how many years
has it stood—and it is silent. Many, many times
has it seen the rising and setting sun, the rains have
washed it, the snows have covered it . . . but still it
stands. For whose delight? Its builders rotted away
in the earth a long time ago, the brilliant mind that
conceived it this way had long crumbled to dust
and the heart that had worried and rejoiced had long
become earth, a handful of earth. What did that
unknown master think leaving behind this light fairy
tale in stone? Was he magnifying God or did he
simply want to show off?

V. M. SHUKSHIN, *The Master*, ca. 1970

*This building, high on its hillside,
guarding the approaches to Moscow,
is silhouetted at sunrise
against the cold winter sky.*

Brook at Abramtsova

Landscape is beauty and beauty is a spiritual category. It is not without reason that, from ancient times, landscape became an object of art, an object of painting, literature and even music. . . .When perceiving nature we unconsciously set into motion the emotional reserves that we have accumulated by reading our poets and writers, through the contemplation of painting, by listening to music. I wish to say that our very feeling for nature is organized, nurtured, traditional, in a word, culture-bound. Each people has had and has its own singers of nature who are, possibly, sometimes little known to other peoples. But if the Earth is our common fatherland and if feeling for this common fatherland is, little by little, developing in us—in the face of the universe's threatening visage—if we come to know that there may be nothing in the whole universe more beautiful than our planet (and our Earth is truly sublime), then we owe this knowledge to our educators: to the artists and to the poets of significance to all mankind who have helped us to understand beauty, who nurtured in us love of nature.

V. A. SOLOUKHIN, *Civilization and Landscape,* 1979

It took two hours to travel through a snowstorm to Abramtsova, Aksakov's estate. In the early 19th century the trip took two days. Most of the great visiting writers and artists followed this route.

The Monastery at Zagorsk

To properly understand the uniqueness of the scene you must be reminded of the orthodox design of every Greek church. The top of these godly monuments is always composed of several towers which vary in form and height, but of which there are always at least five; the sacramental number is sometimes considerably greater. The steeple in the center is the tallest; the four others, placed on lower tiers, surround the principal tower respectfully. Their form varies; the tops of these symbolic turrets often resemble pointed caps placed upon a head; one could also compare the painted and exteriorly gilded main steeple of certain churches to a bishop's mitre, a Chinese pavilion, a minaret, a bronze toque; often, however, it is simply a little cupola shaped like a ball and capped with a point; all of these more or less bizarre forms are crowned with big copper crosses, bejeweled and gilded, the complicated patterns of which faintly recall filigree-work. The number and position of the bell towers always have religious meaning; they signify the ranks of the ecclesiastical hierarchy. It is the patriarch, raising his radiant head between earth and heaven, surrounded by his priests, deacons and subdeacons. Variety, full of fantasy, rules over the design of these more or less ornate roofs, but the primitive purpose, the theological concept, is always respected here. Brilliant chains of gilded or silver-plated metal unite the crosses of the lower spires to the cross of the main tower and this metal filament, stretched over an entire city, produces an effect impossible to render, even in a painting.

MARQUIS DE CUSTINE, *La Russie en 1839*

Zagorsk burst upon us in the sunlight of a brisk winter morning, its presence a memorial to traditional faith.

Snow Field in the Sunrise

Winter had begun long ago. The frost was severe. Disjointed sounds and forms without any visible connection materialized in the frozen haze. They stopped, moved, and disappeared. A crimson sphere was hanging over the forest; not the sun to which we on earth are accustomed, but some other kind, a substitute. As in a dream or a fairy tale, amber-yellow rays, thick as honey, were flowing from it, stiffening in the air and freezing on the trees.

B. L. PASTERNAK, *Doctor Zhivago,* 1957

The roadways leading from Moscow provide impressionistic landscapes, highlighted with snow.

The Manor House at Arkhangelskoe

The manor house was built in the same style as the
church, in the style that is called "Alexandrian" here;
the house was painted yellow too; it had a green
roof, white columns and a pediment with a crest
on it. The local architect had erected both buildings
with the approval of the late Odintsev who could
not stand any, as he called them, frivolous or willful
innovations. Adjacent to the house, on both sides,
were the dark trees of an old-fashioned garden . . .

I. S. TURGENEV, *Fathers and Children*, 1862

*At Prince Yusupov's old palace,
now known as Arkhangelskoe,
in the center of the courtyard,
a cellophane-covered box intrigued us.
We found that it contained
an old statue covered to
protect it from the climate.*

Village Roadway at Pereslavl

Skirting the barn the road turned into the wind and
they drove into a snowdrift. But ahead one could see
an alleyway between two houses so it was obvious
that the snowdrift had been blown onto the road
and that they would have to drive through it. And in
fact, having driven through the snowdrift, they came
out onto a street. Frozen wash, hung up on a line,
fluttered desperately in the wind by the last house:
shirts, one red and one white, pants, leggings and a
skirt. The white shirt flapped especially desperately,
waving its sleeves.

L. N. TOLSTOY, *Master and Man,* 1895

*This village with its frozen
laundry is typical of the small
Russian villages in the
countryside not far from Moscow.*

A Village on the Road to Yaroslavl

The day came, white, clear and cold—the kind on
which you exhale steam and on which hoar frost lies
on the trees, houses and fences. In the village, grey
smoke rose straight up from the chimneys. Beyond
the windows was an abandoned garden. The little
village stood there, pressed down to the ground by
the snow. Further on stretched white fields, a ravine,
and the forest. The sky was white, the air—white,
and the sun did not come out from behind the
white clouds.

B. A. PILNYAK, *Snows, 1920*

*On our way to Yaroslavl,
in the middle of a snow storm,
we paused long enough to
photograph these half-buried houses.*

Winter Pastoral

Everyone prayed for snow just as they pray for rain in the summer and then, finally, wispy clouds appeared in the sky, the cold weakened, the clearness of the blue sky dimmed, a western wind blew up, and a puffy white cloud, approaching imperceptibly, obscured the horizon on all sides. As if having already done its work the wind quieted down and the beneficent snow began to fall straight to the ground, slowly, in big flakes. The peasants joyously watched the downy snowflakes fluttering in the air. At first the flakes fluttered and circled around, then they came to earth. The snow began to fall in the early afternoon and fell uninterruptedly becoming thicker and stronger by the hour. I have always loved to watch snow falling and coming to earth quietly. In order to fully enjoy the tableau I went out into a field and there, before my eyes, was a miraculous sight: the entire limitless space around me had the appearance of a snowy flood, as if the heavens had opened, poured out snowy down, and filled the air with movement and with incredible quiet. The long winter twilight arrived. Falling snow began to cover all things and the earth was clothed in a white murk.

S. T. AKSAKOV, *Sketch of a Winter Day*, 1859

Here we relived memories of our childhood: the thrill of leaving a warm house, all bundled up to play in the soft, new fallen snow.

40

Nekrasov's Estate, Karabikho

Especially that winter the estate was sublime. The
stone posts at the entrance to the court, the snowy
courtyard whose sugary snowdrifts were crisscrossed
by the tracks of sleigh runners, the quiet, the sun,
the sweet smell of smoke from the kitchens in the
sharp frosty air, something cosy, domestic, in the
tracks stamped out between the kitchen and the
house. . . . Quiet and brilliance, the whiteness of the
roofs grown fat with snow, the naked branches
lending a reddish-black hue to the low garden, whose
two sides were visible beyond the house, drowned
in snow as it always was in the winter, our cherished
hundred-year-old spruce raising its sharp greenish-
black crest into the bright blue sky beyond the roof
of the house, beyond its steep pitch which resembled
a snowy mountain peak.

I. A. BUNIN, *The Life of Arsenev,* 1937

*We travelled from Yaroslavl to
Karabikho to the simple estate
of the writer Nekrasov. With its
scattered out-buildings, it is a
typical northern country manor.*

Winter Forest

Gigantic trunks of oaks, lindens, birches, and aspens lie scattered about the forest. First they dry up, then their roots rot out and finally they are battered down by a storm. As they fall they bend and break young neighboring trees which, despite their disfigurement, continue to grow and bloom, picturesquely twisting to the side, stretching toward the ground, or bent into an arch. The corpses of the forest giants, while decaying internally, preserve their external appearance for a long time. Moss and grass grow around the bark. . . . This is a special kind of world and folk fantasy has peopled it with supernatural beings: goblins and wood-sprites.

S. T. AKSAKOV, *Notes of a Rifle Hunter from Orenburg Province,* 1851

Near Klin, the mystery of the Russian winter forest; the inspiration of Shishkin and Tchaikovsky.

Frozen Bank of the Kotorosl, Yaroslavl

Frosts would come—fifty degrees below zero. The snow lay hard and blue. The light rose for only three hours; the rest of the time was night. The sky seemed heavy and it would come down low over the earth. There was silence; only in September the moose bellowed, mating; in December wolves howled; the rest of the time there was the kind of silence that can only exist in a desert.

On a hill by the river stood a village.

A naked incline of brown granite and white slate, wrinkled by wind and water, sloped towards the river. Clumsy brown boats lay on the bank. The river was big, gloomy, cold . . .

B. A. PILNYAK, *A Year of Their Life*, 1915

*Very early one freezing morning,
where the Kotorosl meets the Volga,
we found this fishing boat well
beached in ice.*

Snowscape

This is the kingdom of winter. Everything is covered with snow in the beginning of October. . . . After the first morning frost the trees glisten like a rainbow refracting the sun's rays into a thousand pleasant colors; but it seems that the sun regards winter's devastation with horror; it hardly appears but it is clothed in crimson mist, a harbinger of severe cold. All night long the moon pours out its silvery rays and forms rings in the heavens' clear azure across which shining meteors occasionally fly. There is not even the tiniest breath of wind to disturb the trees which are whitened by hoar frost; they seem spellbound in their new form. 'Tis a wistful but pleasant sight—this extraordinary quiet both in the air and on earth! Silence everywhere!

K. N. BATYUSHKOV, *Excerpts from the Letters of a Russian Officer About Finland*, 1809

Climbing a slippery hillside, we found the shadows of these graceful birches mingled with the crystal reflections of the sun in the snow.

Winter Birches

To understand the poetry of a birch one must go to Russia. This pliant and hardy tree illuminates the depths of the Russian forests with its white moss-marbled trunk. Whether standing alone or commingled with other species, it always enlivens the wood, imparting a bit of its elegant insouciance. Russians love the birch, the "berioza," and I understand their affection. The languid grace of this silvery tree sets it apart from all the others. In summer, when its supple branches arch over its base, or in winter, when its undulating twigs are etched against the white horizon, it is saluted like a friend: "Berioza, berioza."

J. LEGRAS, *Au Pays Russe,* ca. 1895

Through this birch grove we made our way to a small deserted church building. The snow was nature's winter benediction to the scene.

A Courtyard in Yaroslavl

The yard—small, crowded and filled with trash; little sheds, lean-tos and cellars constructed out of wood ends ran from the gates until, twisting away, they ended at a bathhouse. The roofs were piled up with pieces of broken boats, split wood, boards and damp wood chips—the petit bourgeois fished all of this out of the Oka during ice-break or at high-water. And the whole yard was unattractively heaped with piles of various woods. Saturated with water, they rotted in the sun, giving off a smell of decay.

M. GORKY, *Childhood*, 1915

An old lady almost denied us this photograph, but a few soft words and a smile won her cooperation and twenty-five minutes of conversation.

Abandoned Gazebo on the Banks of the Volga

They were not wealthy people. Their house, wooden
but comfortable, a real antique, stood on a hill
amidst a weed-choked garden and an overgrown court-
yard. At the foot of the hill flowed a river, hardly
visible through the thick foliage. From the house a
large terrace led out into the garden and beyond the
terrace lay a beautiful oblong flower-bed, covered
with roses. At the ends of the flower-bed two acacias
were growing. In their youth they had been trained
into a spiral shape by the late owner. A bit further
on, in the depths of a neglected raspberry patch,
stood a gazebo.

I. S. TURGENEV, *Notes of a Hunter*, 1852

*We sensed in this deserted gazebo,
hazy memories of tea in the garden
and summer breezes enjoyed from
the Volga. Today it is a resting
place for the convalescents
of a state sanitorium.*

Pokrov-na-Nerli, near Vladimir

The church Pokrov-na-Nerli is unquestionably the most lyrical, the cleanest and clearest work of the national genius of ancient Rus.

. . . It has stood for eight hundred years, carrying its primordial swan-like beauty through autumn's storms and winter's blizzards.

Andrei Bogolyubsky built it as a celebratory monument to commemorate the victorious expedition of the forces of Vladimir against the Volga Bulgars. Izyaslav, Andrei's young son, did not return from the expedition. Originally, the church's dome was helmet-shaped, so that it might really have looked like a well-proportioned young warrior. Later, an "onion dome" replaced the helmet and now the church stands like a betrothed, snow white, combining elegance and modesty simultaneously.

V. A. SOLOUKHIN, *Native Beauty, 1969*

We walked across rolling meadows and a shaky railroad trestle near Vladimir to seek this unique example of ancient Russian church architecture.

Tolstoy's Birch Avenue at Yasnaya Polyana

Again in the morning, from the big, thickly-foliated birches of the avenue, there is a play of light and shadow on the tall, already dark green grass, and there are forget-me-nots, dead nettles, and everything; most importantly, the swaying of the birches of the avenue is just as it was sixty years ago when I first noticed and came to love this beauty. . .

L. N. TOLSTOY, *Letter to S. A. Tolstoy, 1897*

South from Moscow less than two hundred miles, the road led us to Tolstoy's estate. The doors opened to us as they had to a long parade of artists, savants, and just common folk who travelled there to share the earthy brilliance of this great writer.

Tolstoy's Inheritor

Take a look at the Russian peasant: is there a trace of servile abasement in his gait or his speech? His daring and ingenuity go without saying. His artfulness is well known. His dexterity and adroitness are amazing. A traveller, not knowing a word of Russian, can journey from one end of Russia to the other and everywhere he is understood, his demands are met, agreements are made with him. Amongst our people you will never meet what the French call a "badaud": you will never notice coarse amazement nor an ignorant contempt for the foreign.

A. S. PUSHKIN, *Journey from Moscow to Petersburg*, 1834

This big man is the chief forester at Yasnaya Polyana. Tolstoy would rejoice to know that his trees are being guarded by such a stalwart representative of the Russian tradition.

Turgenev's Linden Walks

The linden walks have become especially beautiful.
I love those walks, I love their grey-green color and
the subtle smell beneath their arches. . . . My favorite
sapling has already become a young oak. Yesterday,
at midday, I sat in its shadow on a bench for more
than an hour. The grass flowered so gaily around me:
a golden hue tinged everything—bright and soft; it
even penetrated the shadow.

I. S. TURGENEV, *Faust*, 1856

*We departed from Moscow and drove
for six hours to the estate of
Turgenev at Spasskoe-Lutovinovo
near Orel. We entered his garden
just as the sun was going down.
Except for the presence of a
large flock of ravens, we were alone.
As we went further into the forest,
we were surrounded by complete silence.*

Ukrainian Pastoral

It seems that you are looking into a bottomless sea, that it spreads out broadly beneath you, that the trees do not rise out of the ground but, instead, descend perpendicularly, falling into the glassy-clear waves like the roots of gigantic plants; the leaves of the trees are, at one moment, transparent like emeralds, then they coalesce into a golden, almost black-green; somewhere, far-far away, a lone leaf rests motionless at the end of a thin branch against a blue patch of the clear sky. . . .White, spherical clouds appear and then float by like magical underwater islands.

I. S. TURGENEV, *Notes of a Hunter*, 1852

*In the Ukraine we were searching
for scenery which had inspired
the great Russian paintings.
It is not surprising that we
also found a Watteau.*

A Ferrous Swamp in the Ukraine

Marshy swamps with mud, with ferrous or rusty and stagnant springs, have a completely different character. . . . The swamp flora is meager. In places you can see circular spots or long belts of watery mud and rather large, sometimes reddish pools. The reddish color of the water and mud indicate the certain presence of iron ore. There are few hummocks and even grass barely grows on the mud and the rusty places; however, they are often overgrown with a thick mane of small reeds, mare's tail and unusually tall sedge. In the rusty pools the surface of the water is covered with a thin film which, in the sun, shines with a ferrous-blue reflection. Water striders love to run back and forth across it on their long, bowed legs. The water in the spring beds, which is sometimes rather deep, has no visible current and merely oozes but it remains fresh and cool even in the summer, especially if you scoop it up from towards the bottom.

S. T. AKSAKOV, *Notes of a Rifle Hunter from Orenburg Province*, 1851

*We looked for Aksakov's swamp
without much success until we
happened to see it through some trees
on the road to Kiev.*

Sunset Reflections at Poltava

Tikhon Pavlovich said, "Stop," got out of the cart and looked around. Forty paces from him a small awkward farmstead was silhouetted against night's gloom: to the right, next to it, was a mill-pond. Its dark water was motionless and was frightening in its immobility. All around it was quiet and scary. The willows on the weir, thickly shrouded in shadow, stood straight up, severely and sternly. Somewhere drops fell. Suddenly, from the grove, a wind came up on the mill-pond; startled, the water rocked and a quiet plaintive splash was audible.

M. GORKY, *Ennui*, 1896

Returning to Poltava, late one afternoon, when light was fast deserting the camera, we came upon a little pond, the tranquility of which soothed us after a hot, dusty Ukrainian day.

Birch Grove

There are few mushrooms here; you have to go into the birch grove for mushrooms, and I am ready to start out. For I never loved anything more in my life than the forest with its mushrooms and wild berries, with its bugs and little birds, hedgehogs and squirrels, with the dank smell of rotten leaves which I love so much. And even now, as I write this, I can smell the birch grove of our village; such impressions last for one's entire life.

F. M. DOSTOEVSKY, *Diary of a Writer: February 1876*

Early one morning, a little path invited investigation. We were walking in and out of one of the great pastoral paintings of the last century.

Vydubetsky Monastery on the Dnieper, Kiev

In the spring the gardens bloomed with white blossoms and the Tsar's garden was cloaked in green. The sun burst through all the windows, lighting fires in them. Ah, Dnieper! Ah, sunsets! Ah, Vydubetsky monastery on the slopes. A terraced green sea rushed down to the varicolored caressing Dnieper. Thick bluish-black nights over the water, the electric cross of St. Vladimir suspended on the heights.

In a word, a sublime city, a happy city. The mother of Russian cities.

M. A. BULGAKOV, *The City—Kiev,* 1923

There are at least six depths of distance in the photograph, any one of which could tell this great monastery's exciting story.

Armenian Mountain Landscape

Armenia is a mountainous land.

Numerous mountain chains, with innumerable slopes, cover the earth's surface, forming a gigantic net. Deep depressions, gloomy canyons, and narrow plains are squeezed between the mountains. These canyons and depressions are separate regions, separated from each other by natural frontiers.

The provinces were isolated and barely communicated with each other. The mountains served as an impassable barrier between them, and the valleys were like deep moats.

Man faced many hardships in the battle with severe nature.

Here there is a precipitous cliff, below is a fathomless depth from which a river's muted rumble is barely audible, and up above rock faces present a constant threat of landslides. Only a native of these mountains, competing in agility with the wild goats, could find his way through such a threateningly savage landscape.

RAFFI, *Samuel,* 1886

*From Kiev we flew to Armenia
and into a land completely
different from anything we had yet
seen in the Soviet Union.*

The Monastery at Gekhard

We clamber up to the ancient cave churches. . . .We enter. Time falls away. The cramped shallow caves with their sooty, uneven walls recall a mine-shaft. I, a former mining engineer, even discovered the traces of bore-holes. Rough niches for icons, small chalices for oblations, a narrow trough for the drainage of blood, the ancient petrified soot of the ceiling, the freshly-scratched names (symbols of a new, touristy era), the contemporary, colored rags (prayers for the recovery of loved ones) and the modern wax of melted candles—such are the stalactites of these caves. What modesty and greatness of belief there is in these poor stone corners. The church was created by nature herself, and the caves are its altars. . . . These caves are the key to the history of the nation. Armenians were massacred as "faithless" but, in fact, they were decimated precisely because of their fidelity —to the land, the language, Christ. They lost their lives but did not lose their homeland. . . . For Armenians the word "Gekhard" is not only the name of a holy place, but also of a general concept. Gekhard is the stronghold of belief. One can explain a lot with the word "Gekhard."

A. G. BITOV, *Armenian Lessons: Gekhard*, 1968

We approached this mountain chapel near Erevan in frigid rain. Once inside the chapel, the carved stone of the interior gave us warmth, both physical and spiritual.

Mount Ararat

After we had driven up onto a hillock above the haze that hung over an endless valley, two mountains suddenly appeared in the distance in front of us. The first one was somewhat closer and of extraordinary height. Neither the immensity of Stefan-Tsmind nor of the other colossi of the Caucasus had so amazed me: together they occupied the greater part of the horizon—this was the two-hilled Ararat. . . . In addition to the recollections that thrill the soul of anyone who reveres the holy legends, the mere sight of that ancient mountain strikes one with indescribable amazement. I stood motionless for a long time.

A. S. GRIBOEDOV, *Travel Notes 1819*

The Cossacks woke me at dawn. My first thought was: am I not feverish? But, thank God, I felt energetic and healthy; there was neither a trace of illness, nor even of fatigue. I went out of the tent into the fresh morning air. The sun was rising. A snowy double-peaked mountain shown white against the clear sky. "What is that mountain?" I asked, stretching forward. In reply I heard: "That is Ararat." How strong the effect of sound is! I looked greedily at the biblical mountain, and saw the ark moored to its summit with hope for renewal and life—ravens and doves flying off, symbols of punishment and reconciliation.

A. S. PUSHKIN, *A Journey to Arzrum, 1835*

*Ararat, forty miles from Erevan,
across the Turkish border,
must be sought in early, early light.
By 7 a.m. the rising mists of Erevan
screen the mountain from view.*

Lake Sevan and the Sevan Monastery

The island of Sevan is notable for two most praise-worthy architectural monuments of the 7th century and also for the earthen huts of some lice-ridden anchorites, who died off not long ago, which are thickly overgrown with nettles and thistles, but which are no scarier than the abandoned basements of country houses. I lived there for a month, enjoying the stationary lake water at four thousand feet and training myself to contemplate two or three dozen tombs scattered about as in a flower-bed among the monastery's dormitories which had been rejuvenated by a repair job.

O. E. MANDELSHTAM, *Journey to Armenia: Sevan*, 1933

Leaving Erevan, the road climbs steeply through rocky terrain, leading onto a plateau which holds a fairy-tale lake surrounded by mountains.

Tbilisi

The houses stuck together, crowded over each other
as if they were seeking an escape from the heat.
Balconies kept the houses apart. On these messy
balconies, enclosed by wooden balustrades, people
dined, cursed, slept and loved, guarding the coolness
like old wine. In the evenings, dully and greedily,
several generations sat here, listening to the goat-like
wail of the Caucasian clarinet. In a blind and pon-
derous craving for reorganization, the typical love of
a soldier, Ermolov ordered the balconies, on which
old Asia was preserved, destroyed. He wanted to
make Tiflis a European city and cut streets like fire
breaks, in military fashion.

 The city fought back . . .

 Ermolov backed down. The city triumphed. Tiflis
was and remained many-balconied.

Yu. N. TYNYANOV, *The Death of Vazir-Mukhtar*, 1929

*Passing from Armenia on our way
to Tbilisi, we crossed the dusty
borders of Azerbaizhan and made
our way into Georgia. Tbilisi,
since the 6th century, has been
its capital. The photograph chronicles
the city's long and turbulent history:
the 4th-century fortress; the 7th-
century cathedral; the 18th- and
19th-century balconied houses.*

Mskheta

Not many years ago,
Where noisily embracing, sister-like,
Conjoin the streams Aragvy and Kury,
A monastery stood. And even now
Beyond the peaks, a passerby
Can see the posts of broken gates
And towers and a church's vault.
The censers' fragrant smoke
No longer curls beneath it,
And late at night the chanting of the monks
Who pray for us is heard no more.
And now an old and grey-haired man,
The half-dead guard of ruins,
From gravestones brushes off the dust,
Forgotten both by men and death.

M. Yu. LERMONTOV, *Mtsyri*, 1840

*High above the valley from an
ancient monastery, a remnant of
the earliest days of Christianity,
we saw the first capital of
Georgia, Mskheta, located at the
confluence of two rivers.*

The Estate of Chavchavadze at Tsinandali

As one gets closer to Telavi the beautiful estates of princes stand out more and more frequently inside their spacious parks on the green knolls.

Tsinandali of Prince Chavchavadze, the most famous of these high-born princes' estates, is eight versts from Telavi. Tsinandali is visible from the road. . . . Tsinandali is renowned for the best Kakhetian wine . . . but it is also a historical curiosity. The last audacious raid of the Chechens into Georgian territory was carried out against it. This was in 1854. No one imagined the possibility of an incursion by the mountain men into the very center of Kakhetia, through the iron band of Russian fortifications and Russian troops . . .

But this is what tempted Shamil's daredevils. They knew that this feat would resound in the most forgotten corners of the Caucasus, that it would seize the peaceful population, who still blindly believed in the Russians' power, with terror . . .

They descended by secret paths, bypassing the guard posts and suddenly, like a bolt out of the blue, they appeared. . . . A crowd of Chechens burst into the house where the women and children of the prince's family had, horrified, locked themselves in . . . half dead from fright the princesses of the old Tsinandali estate were divided up amongst the plunderers.

E. L. MARKOV, *Sketches of the Caucasus*, 1904

In eastern Georgia near Telavi we found an old-fashioned private park once owned by a great writer-prince. It is now a house-museum. The prince's estate boasted at least thirty-five varieties of wine grapes.

Georgian Thunder Storm

The day was a hot, bright, radiant day, despite an
occasional shower. Low, smoky clouds sailed smoothly
across the clear sky without wholly covering the sun
and at times, in a sudden and momentary cloudburst,
they dropped abundant streams on the fields. Heavy,
sparkling, diamond-like drops fell quickly, with a
sort of crisp sound. Sunlight played through their
dancing net and the grass, which had just recently
been rippling in the wind, did not stir as it thirstily
swallowed up the moisture. The leaves of the soaked
trees quivered languidly. The birds never stopped
singing and it was delightful to hear their chattering
twitter together with the hum and murmur of the
passing rain. Dust flew up and the dirt roads became
splotched under the sharp blows of steady drops. But
suddenly the storm cloud passed, the breeze puffed
up, the grass was shot through with emerald and gold.

I. S. TURGENEV, *Rudin*, 1856

*The approaching storm in Beethoven's
Sixth Symphony races across such
a panorama. Thunder and lightning
and, eventually, a drenching
summer rain accompanied us on our
return from Telavi to Tbilisi.*

The Caucasus

Early in the morning, the coolness woke him in his carriage and he glanced indifferently to the right. The morning was absolutely clear. Suddenly, twenty paces away, as it seemed to him at first, he saw clean white masses with their soft outlines and the fantastical, distinct, yet ethereal line where their peaks met the distant sky. And when he realized all the distance between himself, the mountains and sky, the immensity of the mountains, and when he became aware of the endlessness of this beauty, he feared that it was all a mirage, a dream. He shook himself to wake up.

The mountains remained the same . . .

At first the mountains only amazed Olenin, later, he rejoiced in them; but then, staring more and more at the sight, not from other black mountains but straight at the chain of snowy mountains which were running away and growing right out of the steppe, Olenin began, little by little, to enter into that beauty, to *feel* the mountains. From that time on everything that he saw, everything that he thought, everything that he felt, became tinged with the new strongly majestic character of the mountains.

L. N. TOLSTOY, *The Cossacks*, 1863

We left Tbilisi in the cool of the morning and headed north to the Caucasus. We followed the famous Georgian Military Road, an engineering marvel of the early 19th century. Pushkin, Lermontov, and Tolstoy had passed over this road before us.

Caucasian Canyon

The world of the Caucasian alps is made up of a
series of stony nests amongst which roar wild moun-
tain torrents. The furiously roaring river waves are
accompanied only by perpendicular walls, several
thousand feet high, sometimes of granite, sometimes
of slate, sometimes of limestone, but always silent
and hopeless. A deaf and raw twilight hangs over
these uninhabited gorges which are filled with de-
struction, enmity and death. An environment like
this either forges the whole being of a man into inde-
structible steel or it crushes him. There is little room
here for tender emotions or humanitarian strivings.
Solitary brown eagles fly in the heavens, glaring at
each other and exchanging hostile and suspicious
squawks. They kill lambs and chamois on the naked
precipices with their rapacious claws and beaks which
are as sharp as curved daggers.

F. MECH, *The Caucasus*, ca. 1840

*As we climbed into a wild mountain
fastness, we were surrounded by
enormous flocks of sheep being led
to summer pasture. Snow and rock,
and evidence of the slides of both,
lay around us in profusion.*

Fiagdon (The Crazy River), near Ordzhonikidze

From a hill, made of gigantic misshapen rocks glued
together by nature . . . ran a thin stream of water.
It fell to the earth and raced off somewhere to the
left, transparent and merry, sparkling in the sun and
quietly gurgling as if it imagined itself to be a strong
and wild torrent. Not far from the hill the streamlet
spread out into a pool. Broiling rays and the scorched
earth greedily drank up the pool and sapped its
strength; but, a bit further on, it probably flowed
together with another such spring because, a hundred
paces from the hill, along the water course stood a
green, thick, luxuriant hedge.

A. P. CHEKHOV, *Steppe*, 1888

*All their lives Americans look for a
perfect picnic ground. We found it
near Ordzhonikidze in a quiet
little valley shaded by trees beside
the race of the "Crazy" River.*

"Lermontov" Pavilion, Pyatigorsk

Now, magnificent baths and houses have been con-
structed. A boulevard, planted with lindens, has been
laid out along the incline of Mashuk. There are tidy
little paths, green shops, proper flower-beds, little
bridges and pavilions everywhere. The springs have
been done over, lined with masonry. Instructions
from the police have been nailed to the walls of the
baths: everywhere there is order, cleanliness and
beauty. . . . I admit: today the Caucasian spas offer
more amenities, but I miss their former wild state.

A. S. PUSHKIN, *A Journey to Arzrum*, 1835

*Pyatigorsk means five hills.
We came upon this garden town
in the rain. Now populated by
pensioners seeking the health-giving
properties of the local springs,
the place was stylish one hundred
and fifty years ago. It leans
heavily on its original monuments.*

Wheat Fields with Poppies, Crimea

Summer arrived in the space of a week.

   The last migratory bird appeared and built its
nestlet. Red and white poppies burst into bloom.
Baby-blue flowers of silken flax poured like a sea over
the field. White buckwheat peppered the whole
endless path like powdery snow. . . . The linden
gleamed like a solid gold arrow while the silvery oats
and pale-amber wheat spread hither and yon. They
covered the forests and ravines; infinitely stretching
to the deep blue sky, and they were lost in the hum-
ming and abundance of pre-harvest insatiability.

A. M. REMIZOV, *The Black Rooster*, 1907

*One of the great surprises of our
whole trip was the rolling plain
north of Yalta. The wheat fields
were filled with wild flowers,
splashed with radiant red poppies
as far as the eye could see.*

The Black Sea at Gurzuf, near Yalta

In Gurzuf I went nowhere, swam in the sea and gorged myself on grapes. I became used to the southern environment immediately and enjoyed it with all the indifference and insouciance of a Neapolitan *lazzaroni*. Waking at night, I loved to hear the sound of the sea and I listened spellbound for hours. Two paces from our house a young cypress was growing; each morning I visited it and became attached to it with a feeling resembling friendship. That is all I remember of my stay in Gurzuf.

A. S. PUSHKIN, *Letter to Delvig, 1824*

The weather here is warm and absolutely summerlike. . . . I walked without a coat and even so it's hot. The Crimean coast is beautiful and cozy, and I like it better than the Riviera; there's only one problem — no civilization. In Yalta, as far as civilization goes, they've moved even further than Nice: there is excellent plumbing here, but the environs are positively Asiatic.

A. P. CHEKHOV, *Letter to A. S. Suvorin Oct. 8, 1898: Yalta*

The delights of the Crimea quickly became evident: a land of palaces, mountains, forests, streams, lakes, and a wide expanse of open sea. Little coves abound.

The Khan's Palace at Bakhchisarai

Yesterday evening I approached Bakhchisarai and descended into the gorge in which it lies. Before nightfall I was able only to travel along the long street leading to the Khansarai (that is, to the Khan's palace), which is found on the eastern edge of the city. When I entered the first building of the sarai the sun had long disappeared behind the mountains and dusk had begun to deepen. This did not prevent me from racing through the towers and palaces of this Tauride Alhambra; as objects became less visible, my imagination, filled with the iridescent colors of eastern poetry, played more vividly . . .

When I describe one of the chambers of the upper living quarters to you, you will have an idea of all the others, which differ one from another only in having a greater or lesser amount of decoration on the walls . . .

There is but one entrance to the chamber, an inconspicuous side door between pilasters in the Arabian style. Between the pilasters there are also cabinets, equally inconspicuous, which run along the dark wall of the chamber. Above them (in the best chambers), up to the ceiling inside and out, are windows, between which are carved decorations: bowls with fruits and with flowers or little trees with figures of various birds. The ceilings are the same as the dark wall: joinery and exceptionally beautiful work. . . . In addition to shutters, stained patterned glass in the windows, the favorite decoration of knights' castles which was doubtless borrowed by the Europeans from the eastern peoples during the Crusades, serves to protect the rooms (which are lighted from three sides) from the bright rays. If, to conclude this general description, you imagine a divan (that is, pillows made of silken cloth) lying on the floor along all the walls except the dark one, you will have an idea of the best halls of the palace.

I. M. MURAV'EV-APOSTOL, *A Journey in Tauride*, 1823

No man breathes who has not fancied life in a harem. We found this one in the Khan's palace at Bakhchisarai, north of Yalta. The old building was the center of severe fighting. To many, the struggle was to secure the Khanate for Catherine the Great. To others, it may have been to realize a dream.

The Peter and Paul Fortress, Leningrad

Petersburg looks like an oval and occupies a gigantic
territory. It is still not fully built in many places; but
if the tsar remains alive long the spaces will quickly
be filled up. The St. Petersburg fortress, where the
bell-tower is located, is built right on the Neva and
has several thick and tall stone bastions studded with
a large number of cannon. They say that its fortifi-
cation, which was done in great haste, cost a multitude
of lives and that, due to the unusual dearness of food-
stuffs and deficiencies in clothing, people died like
flies from cold and hunger and were buried right
there . . .

The whole left side of the river, where the fortress
stands, consists of a single continuous mass such that
you can walk from one end to the other on dry land.
But the city, where the Admiralty is, along the right
bank of the river, is divided up by many canals over
which bridges have been placed.

F. W. BERGHOLZ, *Diary of a Kammer-Junker, July 1721*

*In Leningrad we immediately
became part of its baroque life:
concerts, art museums, palaces,
gardens, and an old hotel which
had been the host to kings.*

Leningrad, Venice of the North

I love you, Peter's work,
Your stern severe appearance.
I love the Neva's regal flow
The granite of its banks,
The patterns of your iron gates,
Your pensive nights
Transparent twilight, moonless gleam
When in my room I write
And read without a light.
The sleeping hulks of empty streets
Are clear, the spire of
The Admiralty is bright.
And not permitting dark of night
To mar the golden heavens,
One dawn succeeds another,
Allowing night a hurried half an hour.

A. S. PUSHKIN, *The Bronze Horseman*, 1833

*We wandered late into the white night.
Having turned a corner, at the
Hermitage we found this view of
the Neva River. Tchaikovsky
evidently turned this corner too.
It is a scene in his operatic
tragedy, "Pique Dame."*

St. Isaac's Cathedral, Leningrad

The Isaac Church faces the Neva, and, when completed, will be one of the grandest in the world. The original one was founded by Peter the Great: this by Catherine was not considered sufficiently handsome, and she ordered that it should be rebuilt in marble; but the late Emperor not approving of the manner in which it had been finished, gave orders for it to be rased; and the present pile was commenced. It is to be in the form of a Greek cross, with a dome in the centre, the ball of which will be three hundred feet from the ground. The four porticos consist of columns fifty-six feet high and of one block of granite: the raising of these, and placing them in their relative situations, is a most interesting sight. Under sheds there are constantly hundreds of workmen employed polishing these immense pillars, and lightening their labour with the song.

J. E. ALEXANDER, *Travels to the Seat of War in the East*, 1830

The Isaac Church was just outside the window of our hotel on the Isaac Square. This square was famous for a second reason. The revolutionary Decembrists in 1825 made their brief and futile stand here.

The Alexander Column, Leningrad

The Neva was rising . . . finally a thunderstorm blew
in; lightening bolt after lightening bolt, flaming up
in a thousand places, as if they stood over the city.
Some, like serrated arrows, crossed in the sky, others
blazed like crimson shafts . . . buildings, roofs and
towers would appear and then vanish in the darkness
and the swaying masts of sailing ships stood out in
the bright light. The mass of the column gleamed
and would suddenly come completely out of the
darkness to throw a momentary shadow on the square
which was illuminated around it. Then, together,
they would vanish, only to shine once more and
disappear.

V. A. ZHUKOVSKY, *Memories of the Celebration of August 30, 1834*

*Although this column was raised
to an emperor in the Palace Square,
it marks the scene of revolutionary
exploits (1905 and 1917)
which shook the modern world.*

Old House at Lisy Nos (Fox's Nose), near Leningrad

He arrived early in the morning and the first thing that struck him as he drove into the yard was the neglected and decrepit appearance of the buildings and, particularly, of the house. The iron roof, which had once been green, had not been painted for a long time and was red with rust. Several shingles were twisted up, probably by a storm. The boards with which the house was sided had been torn off in places. People had torn them off where they came off easily, by pulling out the rusty nails. The porches—both of them: the one in front and the one in back that he particularly remembered—had rotted through and were broken down. Only the frames remained. Several of the windows had been boarded over with planks instead of glass.

L. N. TOLSTOY, *Resurrection*, 1896

*The tales old dachas have to tell
invite attention from every window.
Not far from Leningrad
we found our story house.*

The Abandoned Orlov Palace on the Gulf of Finland

The manor-house began to appear, bit by bit, and
finally it looked out in its entirety from the place
where the chain of cottages broke off and where, in
their place, there was merely an orchard or cabbage
patch gone to seed and surrounded by a fence, low
and twisted in places. That strange, elongated, exces-
sively elongated castle looked like some kind of
decrepit invalid. In some places it was of one story,
in others of two. From the dark roof, which did not
completely succeed in defending the house's old age,
stuck two belvederes, facing each other, both of them
already tottering and devoid of the paint that had
once covered them. In places the walls of the house
were cracked through to the naked plaster frame and
it was obvious that they had suffered severely from
all sorts of bad weather, rains, whirlwinds and autumn
weather shifts. Of the windows only two were open.
The rest were shuttered or even closed over with boards.

N. V. GOGOL', *Dead Souls*, 1842

Dimly through the falling snow,
we spotted a decaying palace of the past.
A little dog was barking loudly
as if to draw our attention to more
modern problems or to keep us
from going through the broken fence.

Pine Forest at Repino

A pine forest —ancient and old-fashioned, with bears'
dens, with grey shaggy mosses, redolent of resin and
mushrooms. It has seen the iron helms of princely
hosts, and the cowls of old mendicants, true believers,
and the tattered caps of Razin's outlaw band, and
the frozen plumes of Napoleon's Frenchies. And—
they have all passed by, as if they never were. Once
more—blue wintry days, the rustle of snow-covered
switches—a hearty frosty crack down the twigs. A
woodpecker taps; yellow summery days, waxen candles
in twisted green hands, transparent copper tears along
tough gnarled trunks; cuckoos reckon the years.

E. I. ZAMYATIN, *Rus,* 1927

*The great artist Repin lived in this
forest. His paintings of people,
for which he was famous, are timeless.
Again and again, we remarked these
types as we passed them on the street.*

Snow Storm

The morning was dull lilac, as if the world was illuminated by invisible well-camouflaged streetlights with porcelain lilac-colored shades. The snow, stretching endlessly in all directions, was lilac, the hoar frost on the birches (the lilac tinge of their trunks) was lilac, the clouds, behind which the sun would appear any minute now, were also lilac. I would not have been surprised if a lilac orb had floated into the sky from beyond the snow.

V. A. SOLOUKHIN, *A Winter Day,* 1974

On crunching ice with the wind howling and blowing snow in every direction, we crawled out onto a bridge to capture this moment. In the summertime we returned to find this place a calm and beautiful lake.

Sunset during White Nights

The sunset glowed in the distance.

Julia imagined that she herself was walking over the bridge, then along the path, further and further, and all around it was quiet; sleepy rails squawked and a fire winked in the distance. And suddenly, for some reason, it seemed to her that she had seen these very same clouds which stretched over the red part of the sky, the forest and the field, had seen them long ago and often. She felt herself alone and wished to walk and walk and walk along the path; and there, where the twilight glowed, rested the reflection of something other-worldly, eternal.

A. P. CHEKHOV, *Three Years*, 1895

We found that trees do not have to be big to be beautiful in the sunset. This sunset took place at midnight on the Gulf of Finland.

Wild Flowers

I returned home through the fields. It was the very middle of summer. They had already harvested the meadows and were just preparing to cut the rye.

There is a wonderful assortment of flowers at that time of year: red, white, pink, perfumed and fluffy clover; impudent daisies; "loves me, loves me not," milk-white with bright yellow centers and with its musty, heady odor; yellow rocket with its honey-like smell; tall lilac and white tulip-shaped harebells; creeping vetch; yellow, red, pink, lilac, tidy scabiosa; plantain, with its slightly pink down and faint pleasant smell; cornflowers, bright blue in the sunlight when they are young, pale blue with some red in the evening as they get old; and delicate dodders, which wilt immediately, with their almondy smell.

L. N. TOLSTOY, *Hadzhi-Murat*, 1905

Flowers mean much to the Russians,
wild flowers particularly.
For no reason at all, other than
to be pleasant, someone presents you
with a little bouquet and a good wish.

The Smolensk Cemetery, Leningrad

In one of the distant corners of Russia there is a small
village cemetery. Like almost all our cemeteries it is
a melancholy sight. The ditches which surround it
have long been overgrown, the grey wooden crosses
have bent sideways and rot underneath their once-
painted coverings; the stone slabs have been displaced,
as if someone is pushing them from below. . . . But
among them there is one that no one touches, which
is not trampled on by animals; only the birds sit on
it and sing at sunrise.

I. S. TURGENEV, *Fathers and Children*, 1862

*An abandoned Leningrad
cemetery shelters memories
of the almost forgotten past.*

The Pushkin Monument at Pushkin

Pushkin's monument was not Pushkin's monument,
. . . but simply Pushkin-Monument, in a single word,
with equally incomprehensible and individually non-
existent comprehensions of Pushkin and monument.
. . . Pushkin's monument was the goal and the
boundary of a walk: from Pushkin's monument —
to Pushkin's monument. Pushkin's monument was
also the goal of a run: whoever gets to Pushkin's
monument first . . . Pushkin's monument was an
everyday item—the same kind of character in a child's
life as the piano or the policeman Ignatev outside
the window.

M. I. TSVETAEVA, *My Pushkin*, 1937

*Not all monuments to the past
are deserted. On Pushkin's
birthday, June 6, his statues
are covered with flowers.*

Ancient Oak in the Tsar's Garden

"Yes, here in this forest was that oak . . . hmm where is it?"—Prince Andrei thought again; looking to the left side of the road and, not knowing what he was doing, not recognizing it, he was admiring the very oak for which he had been searching. The old oak, having spread a canopy of lush green foliage, was completely transformed and it stood solidly, barely swaying in the rays of the evening sun. . . . Succulent young leaves pushed straight through the tough, hundred-year-old bark in such a way that it was impossible to believe that this greybeard had produced them.

L. N. TOLSTOY, *War and Peace*, 1869

In the Tsar's forest at Tsarskoe Selo (now Pushkin), there are many old trees of long memory, delightful little waterways and ornate bridges. The secrets of this wood are no longer kept.

Wooden Churches at Kizhi

Kizhi—a churchyard right on the bank of Lake Onega. There is no nearby village, only churches and the cabins of clergymen. There are two churches: one, with twenty-two cupolas, constructed either at the very end of the seventeenth or at the very beginning of the eighteenth century, and the other, also a very interesting one with nine cupolas, built during the reign of Catherine the Great. . . . Towards dusk, in the deepening twilight, the silhouettes of these churches present an enchanting spectacle against the background of an inextinguishable northern summer sunset. What a master it must have been who built such churches!

The basic principle of Russian antique wooden architecture is that the parts never overbalance the whole—first priority is the overall shape. If a structure is fanciful then it is first of all fanciful in its general contours as, for example, the churches of Kizhi. Ornamentation in just a few places, like a pretty vignette at the end of a text, gently accentuates the structure's general loveliness. There is no ornamentation which lacks some practical structural value . . .

One can, on the whole, say the same things about the peasant cottage as about the wooden church because both have the same creator: the people.

I. Ya. BILIBIN, *Folk Art of Northern Russia*, 1904

These wooden churches, identical in origin with the Scandinavian Stavkyrka, are located on an island some three hundred miles north of Leningrad. They are built on the site of a pagan place of worship, as was Notre Dame of Paris.

The Mirozhsky Monastery, Pskov

For the city is whole to this very day—with its marble walls, golden-domed churches, noble monasteries, ornamented princely towers, with the boyars' stone palaces, and its houses hewn from incorruptible beams. The city is whole, but invisible. It was hidden miraculously by God's command when the godless Khan came to conquer the Principality. He wanted to put the houses to the torch, to kill the men, and to take the women and girls hostage. But the Lord did not allow the infidel to desecrate this Christian holy place. Ten days and ten nights the Khan's hordes searched for the city: and they could not find it for they had been blinded. And to this day the city remains invisible. But of a quiet summer evening, one can see walls, churches, mountains, princely towers, boyar mansions, and the houses of tradespeople reflected in the water. And at night one can hear the muffled, mournful knell of the bells.

"Legend of the City of Kitezh" (adapted from the version of
P. I. MELNIKOV-PECHERSKY, *"In the Forests"*, 1875)

Seen dimly through the haze, an old monastery as ancient as its faith lives out its days beside the peaceful Velikaya River at Pskov.

Pushkin's Lake at Mikhailovskoe

. . . I visited once more
the little corner of the earth where I,
An exile, passed two unnoticed years.
Ten years have gone since then and much
In life has changed for me. I too, submissive
To the common law, have changed, but here
Again past days envelop me
So vividly. It seems but yestereve
I wandered in these groves . . .
Just there's the wooded hill, on which betimes
I'd sit quite motionless and glance
Upon the lake—while wistfully recalling
Other shores and other waves.
Dark blue, it stretches broadly out,
Amidst the golden fields and pastures green . . .

A. S. PUSHKIN, 1835

Near Pskov, the site of Pushkin's exile is kept as he left it. Though he would rather have been in Petersburg, he found constant inspiration here which became part of the beauty of his writing.

L'Envoi

In these photographs we see only a small part of the face of old Russia, no less mysterious, no less intriguing, no less beautiful today than at the dawn of its long history.

How like Vermont and Connecticut. How like Colorado and the forests of Ohio. How like the lakes of Minnesota and Wisconsin. How like the canyons of the Rocky Mountains.

At first, not finding in our photographs the *uniquely* Russian, but more of *us* than we had expected, we thought success in recreating the mystery of Russia had eluded us. Slowly it came to our consciousness that the planet serves up nature's same gifts and, with beneficence, provides for us all.

The human spirit is the same, although we find superficial differences between the north and south, the east and west.

The distance which our camera has brought so close should stir deep within us a recognition of ourselves and of *our* home place.

Nothing is presented here that cannot be seen by anyone, not one place is visited that cannot be found

Proctor Jones and Andrew Wachtel at Pushkin

by any willing traveler. In no corner was the extended hand ignored, and, with a smile, no traveler should find it different.

The true wealth of any land is in its people and in its countryside. So much was laid before us and so little of what became ours can be reproduced here. So take these limited tokens as representative of the whole.

But see that no gem, no ore, no river's force is unique. The makings of a universal life abound on all sides, asking only useful understanding.

Caucasian Shepherd and Flock

Index

*The Mikhailovsky Park on the
Moika River, Leningrad*

Bibliography

Aksakov, S. T. *Sobranie sochinenii v pyati tomakh*. Vols. 2, 5. Moskva: Pravda, 1966.

Alexander, J. E. *Travels to the Seat of War in the East*. London: H. Colborn and R. Bentley, 1830.

Batyushkov, K. N. *Opyty v stikhakh i proze*. Moskva: Nauka, 1977.

Bergholz, F. W. *Dnevnik kammer-yunkera*. 2nd. ed. Moskva: Katkov, 1858-62.

Bilibin, I. Ya. "Narodnogo tvorchestvo russkogo severa." *Mir iskusstva*, #11, 1904.

Bitov, A. G. *Obraz zhizni*. Moskva: Molodaya gvardiya, 1972.

Bulgakov, M. A. *Sobranie sochinenii v desyati tomakh*. Vol. 1. Ann Arbor: Ardis, 1982-___.

Bunin, I. A. *Sobranie sochinenii v desyati tomakh*. Vol. 6. Moskva: Khudozhestvennaya literatura, 1966.

Chekhov, A. P. *Polnoe sobranie sochinenii i pisem*. Works, Vols. 7, 9. Letters, Vol. 7. Moskva: Nauka, 1974-82.

Custine, A. L. L. *La Russie en 1839*, Bruxelles: Wouters et ce., 1843.

Dostoevsky, F. M. *Polnoe sobranie sochinenii v tridtsati tomakh*. Vol. 22. Leningrad: Nauka, 1972-___.

Gogol', N. V. *Sobranie khudozhestvennykh proizvedenii v pyati tomakh*. Vol. 5. Moskva: Akademiya nauk, 1960.

Gorky, M. *Sobranie sochinenii v tridtsati tomakh*. Vols. 2, 13. Moskva: Gosizdat, 1949-55.

Griboedov, A. S. *Polnoe sobranie sochinenii*. Vol. 3. Petrograd: Akademiya nauk, 1917.

Legras, J. *Au pays russe*. 2nd ed. Paris: A. Colin et cie., 1900.

Lermontov, M. Yu. *Sobranie sochinenii v chetyrekh tomakh*. Vols. 3, 4. Leningrad: Nauka, 1981.

Mandelshtam, O. E. *Sobranie sochinenii v chetyrekh tomakh*. Vol. 2. Paris: Inter-language Literary Associates, 1964-81.

Markov, E. L. *Ocherki Kavkaza*. 2nd. ed. St.-Petersburg: Vol'f, 1904.

Melnikov-Pechersky, P. I. *V lesakh*. Moskva: Gosizdat, 1955.

Murav'ev-Apostol, I. M. "Puteshestvie po Tavride," in *Bakhchisaraisky fontan*. St.-Petersburg: Suvorin, 1892.

Pasternak, B. L. *Doktor Zhivago*. Rome: Feltrinelli, 1957.

Pilnyak, B. A. *Byl'e*. Munchen: Fink Verlag, 1970.

———. *Rasplesnutoe vremya, Rasskazy*. Chicago: Russian Language Specialties, 1966.

Pushkin, A. S. *Polnoe sobranie sochinenii v desyati tomakh*. Vols. 3, 4, 6, 7,. Moskva: Akademiya Nauk, 1962-66.

Raffi. *Samuel; istorichesky roman*. Moskva: 1946.

Remizov, A. M. *Izbrannoe*. Moskva: Khudozhestvennaya literatura, 1978.

Shukshin, V. M. *Rasskazy*. Moskva: Russky Yazik, 1981.

Soloukhin, V. A. *Izbrannye proizvedenniya v dvukh tomakh*. Vol. 2. Moskva: Khudozhestvennaya literatura, 1974.

———. *Rodnaya krasota*. London: Iskander, 1969.

———. *Vremya sobirat' kamni*. Moskva: Sovremennik, 1980.

Tolstoy, L. N. *Sobranie sochinenii*. Vols. 3-7, 12-14. Moskva: Gosizdat, 1960-65.

Tsvetaeva, M. I. *Sobranie sochinenii v dvukh tomakh*. Vol. 2. Moskva: Khudozhestvennaya literatura, 1980.

Turgenev, I. S. *Polnoe sobranie sochinenii i pisem*. Vols. 4, 6, 7, 8. Moskva-Leningrad: Nauka, 1960-68.

Tynyanov, Yu. N. *Sobranie sochinenii v trekh tomakh*. Moskva-Leningrad: Gosizdat, 1959.

Zamyatin, E. I. *Nechestivye rasskazy*. Leningrad: Krug, 1927.

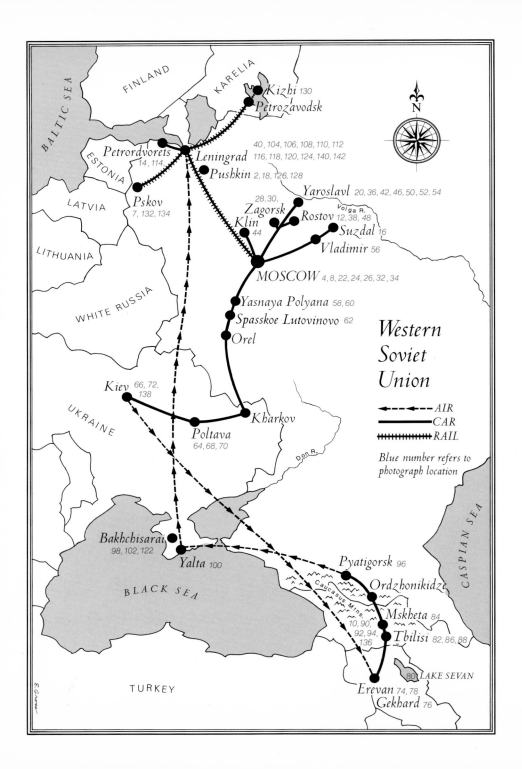

Kizhi 130
Petrozavodsk

Petrordvorets 14, 114
Leningrad 40, 104, 106, 108, 110, 112
116, 118, 120, 124, 140, 142
Pushkin 2, 18, 126, 128

Pskov 7, 132, 134

Yaroslavl 20, 36, 42, 46, 50, 52, 54

28, 30,
Zagorsk
Klin 44 **Rostov** 12, 38, 48
Suzdal 16
Vladimir 56

MOSCOW 4, 8, 22, 24, 26, 32, 34

Yasnaya Polyana 58, 60
Spasskoe Lutovinovo 62
Orel

Western Soviet Union

Kiev 66, 72, 138

Poltava 64, 68, 70

Kharkov

← — ← — AIR
————— CAR
╫╫╫╫╫╫ RAIL

Blue number refers to photograph location

Bakhchisarai 98, 102, 122
Yalta 100

Pyatigorsk 96
Ordzhonikidze
Mskheta 84
10, 90,
92, 94, **Tbilisi** 82, 86, 88
136

80 LAKE SEVAN

Erevan 74, 78
Gekhard 76

FINLAND
KARELIA
BALTIC SEA
ESTONIA
LATVIA
LITHUANIA
WHITE RUSSIA
UKRAINE
Volga R.
Don R.
BLACK SEA
Caucasus Mtns.
CASPIAN SEA
TURKEY

E. Garnet

Book design by Adrian Wilson
Production management by Edmond Gross

Text set by Mackenzie-Harris Corp. in Centaur and Arrighi.
Display type set at The Press in Tuscany Alley in Michelangelo,
Palatino, and Palatino Italic

Laser scanned color separations, photolithography and binding
executed by Dai Nippon Printing Co., Ltd., Tokyo, Japan

ISBN: 0-9608860-3-6
Library of Congress Catalogue Number: 84-90697

*Proctor Jones Publishing Co.**
3401 Sacramento Street
San Francisco, CA 94118

**Photographs are available through the publisher*